KU-593-844

GREAT BRITONS

ENGINEERS

Moira Butterfield

FRANKLIN WATTS

LONDON•SYDNEY

First published in 2007 by
Franklin Watts

Copyright © Franklin
Watts 2007

Franklin Watts
338 Euston Road
London NW1 3BH

Franklin Watts Australia
Level 17/207 Kent Street
Sydney, NSW 2000

All rights reserved.

A CIP catalogue record for
this book is available from
the British Library.

Dewey number: 620.0092

ISBN: 978 0 7496 7470 0

Printed in China

Franklin Watts is a division
of Hachette Children's
Books, an Hachette Livre
UK company.

Designer: Thomas Keenes
Art Director: Jonathan Hair
Editor: Sarah Ridley
Editor-in-Chief:
John C. Miles
Picture Research:
Diana Morris

Picture credits:
Alinari/Topfoto: 31.
British Library/HIP/
Topfoto: 25. Mary Evans
Picture Library: 15, 27.
Fortean Picture
Library/Topfoto: 7.
Fotomas/Topfoto: 10, 13,
23. John Hedgecoe/
Topfoto: 39.
PA/Topham: 32, 43.
Picturepoint/Topham: 9, 28,
37.
Science Photo Library: 21.
Time & Life Pictures/Getty
Images: 35.
Topfoto: front cover, 17,
18, 40.
UPP/Topfoto: 45.

Every attempt has been
made to clear copyright.
Should there be any
inadvertent omission
please apply to the
publisher for rectification.

CONTENTS

INTRODUCTION

The twenty men in this book have changed the way people live, not just in Britain but all around the world. Their work, and the work of many others, has made Britain justly world-famous as a centre of creative engineers with innovative ways of thinking.

It was engineers who made the Industrial Revolution possible in Britain. Factories, steam engines, canals, modern roads and metal bridges brought about a complete change in the way people worked and travelled. All these ideas started in Britain but spread across the world.

Many of the people in this book came from poor backgrounds, and were perhaps never expected to do important work. But they had a spirit of curiosity which drove them forward. They never gave up on their work, however hard it sometimes seemed to be to make progress. Many of them invented not just one engineering marvel in their life, but many.

There are not yet any British women engineers famous enough to be 'household names'. That is very likely to change in the 21st century. In the past, women were not given an engineering education or given credit for new inventions, but in the modern age they are just as likely to succeed.

Unlike many of the famous figures in this book, modern engineers tend to work in teams, so no one person takes the credit for the work. But just because modern engineers are not quite so well known does not mean they are not inventing new things. British engineers are still doing all kinds of ground-breaking work in the modern world.

The characters in this book are all very different from each other but between them they prove that engineering is anything but dull. Engineers have the power to change people's lives, change whole civilisations, and even change the entire world!

ROBERT HOOKE
A MAN OF MANY TALENTS

BORN Freshwater, Isle of Wight, 18 July 1635
DIED London, 3 March 1703
AGE 67 years

Robert Hooke was a 17th century engineer, and also an expert in science, biology and astronomy. He even helped redesign the layout of London after the Great Fire. He is famous for inventing 'Hooke's joint', still in use today.

As a boy Hooke showed how practical he was by making mechanical toys for a hobby. When he was 13 he was sent to London to be the pupil of a portrait painter, but he turned out to be allergic to paint. He was sent to Westminster School instead, where it seems he could not stop inventing. One of his teachers wrote that he had 'contrived several ways of flying' while he was still at school.

The Age of Reason

Robert Hooke lived at an exciting time in Britain, when many scientists and philosophers were coming up with new inventions and theories. This period is sometimes called the Age of Reason, because scientific theories based on reasoning and experimentation began to gain in importance over previous theories based on interpretations of the Bible.

Hooke went to work for the Royal Society, a newly created academy of science where the greatest minds of the day swapped ideas and gave talks. Soon he became one of its brightest members. Among his many achievements, he designed London churches and even discovered a new star in space.

His best-known engineering triumph was the invention of a type of joint, called a 'Hooke's joint'. It was a simple idea that made a great deal of difference to transport. It meant that a long rod could move in the middle, so that it could connect different parts of a machine that were not in line with each other. It is still used hundreds of years later in modern vehicles, on the driveshaft that connects up different sections underneath the chassis (body).

Hooke was a difficult man and he argued with other well-known scientists of the day. He fell out badly with Isaac

An artist's impression of Robert Hooke. He was a brilliant but often a difficult character.

Newton (1642-1727), who discovered gravity, when he accused Newton of stealing his ideas. We have no pictures of Hooke but it was said that he stooped badly, after many years spent hunched over his work. 🇬🇧

ABRAHAM DARBY THE FIRST

THE FATHER OF THE INDUSTRIAL REVOLUTION

BORN Wren's Nest, near Birmingham, 1678
DIED Madeley Court, Worcestershire, 8 March 1717
AGE 39 years

Abraham Darby discovered how to make large quantities of iron by heating iron ore with coal in a furnace. His work triggered the start of the Industrial Revolution. Coal furnace fires soon powered factories across Britain, and eventually throughout the world.

Darby's family followed the religion of the Society of Friends (the Quakers). This connection was to help Darby later on because wealthy Quaker businessmen helped to fund his work.

The Industrial Revolution

The Industrial Revolution was a period in the 18th and 19th centuries when factories sprung up in Britain, employing many people to mass-produce goods. Through selling its goods, Britain became one of the world's wealthiest countries and an important military power.

The Industrial Revolution led to a complete change in the way people lived their lives. Before Darby was born, men and women lived and worked mainly in villages or small towns. By the year 1800 many lived in large cities and went to work in factories.

Darby was taught at home and then became an apprentice (trainee) metalworker. He moved to Bristol and set up the Baptist Mills Brass Works, making different types of brass and iron goods. In those days there were few industrial sites and most people worked in or near their homes.

Darby worked out how to make lots of metal objects that looked just the same, using one mould. Before this innovation, each metal object had to be crafted by hand. This was the start of mass-production, the making of many identical items in a factory, which is how most goods are manufactured today. Darby also worked out how to manufacture complicated brass and iron shapes, without which steam engines could not have been built.

Darby's most important breakthrough came when he set up a brass and iron works in Shropshire. To make iron, iron ore is dug up and then heated in a furnace to make it melt, separating out the useful metal from the rest. Prior to Darby the iron ore was heated with charcoal (burnt wood), which was in very short supply and didn't get very hot. Darby tried using a type of coal in larger furnaces, and found he was able to make iron in much bigger quantities. This helped Britain to become the most successful 19th century industrial power in the world. ⚒

A view of Abraham Darby's ironworks at Coalbrookdale, Shropshire.

JAMES WATT
THE DEVELOPER OF THE STEAM ENGINE

BORN Greenock,
Scotland,
18 January 1736
DIED Heathfield,
England,
19 August 1819
AGE 83 years

The Industrial Revolution was only made possible when James Watt developed the power to drive its machinery and factories. By the time of his death, his steam engines were in use up and down the land.

Watt was born into a merchant's family in Scotland, and was taught mainly at home by his mother. He proved very practical and good at maths so, at 17, he set off for Glasgow to learn how to be a maker of mathematical instruments, used in those days for measuring and for making calculations.

Horsepower

Watt compared the power of his engines to horses, which were used for the same type of work. His machines were described as having horsepower. A 20-horsepower engine could pull as much as 20 horses. Watt worked out how much money he was saving his customers in horse teams, and once they bought one of his engines he charged them a third of that figure every year for 25 years, making himself very rich. Horsepower is still used today to measure engine power.

At first Watt found it hard to set up a business, but eventually he was lucky enough to get a workshop at the University of Glasgow. The professors helped him in his work, and asked him to repair their Newcomen steam engine. The Newcomen steam engine was the first-ever commercial steam engine. It used pressurised steam to push a piston back and forth inside a cylinder, and it was used for pumping water out of mines. It wasn't very efficient, and Watt worked out how he could make it work much better. He added a separate section to the engine called a condenser, and that made it four times as powerful.

Watt then improved the engine even more to make it turn a crank round and round, instead of just pumping something up and down. Now it was useful for all kinds of jobs, such as weaving, grinding and milling. By 1800 there were over 500 of Watt's machines in mines and factories across Britain.

When Watt died he was a very wealthy man. He owned the patent (legal licence) for his steam engine, which meant only his company could sell it. His invention made steam trains and steamboats possible and meant that factories no longer needed to use either horses or water power to turn their machinery. Watt remains world-famous to this day, and the unit of electrical power, the Watt, is named after him.

James Watt was not the inventor of the steam engine, but he improved it and became rich.

JOHN MacADAM
THE CREATOR OF MODERN ROADS

BORN Ayr, Scotland,
21 September 1756
DIED Moffat, Scotland,
26 November 1836
AGE 70 years

We have John MacAdam to thank for our smooth modern roads. His innovations made once-dangerous rutted tracks into well-drained surfaces, and helped to bring about modern travel.

The father of modern roads nearly died as a young child; he was rescued by a nurse when his family's Scottish house burnt to the ground!

MacAdam travelled to the USA when he was 14 and went on to make his fortune during the War of Independence (1775-83). He was a business agent for

LE MACAL

Entretien des Vo,

the British side against the Americans, who were fighting for independence from Britain. When the British lost, he had to leave the country quickly, leaving most of his wealth behind. MacAdam went back to Scotland, where he began to follow a lifelong ambition, experimenting to find new ways of making roads.

Eventually MacAdam got a job in charge of the roads around Bristol and set about remaking them. Instead of the usual jumble of loose stones, he used crushed stone and gravel on top of a firm base of larger stones, all squashed down with a heavy iron roller. He made sure the road was slightly curved upwards in the

Before and after MacAdam

Before MacAdam's improvements, the stones on roads were loose, and were quickly damaged or driven into ruts that could topple a horsedrawn coach. Roads were easily flooded, too. MacAdam's road surface meant that coaches could travel much faster, and no longer had to contend with flooding and dangerous holes. Travel became swifter and safer.

centre (called a camber) so the rain would drain off it into ditches at the side. Roads built this way were said to be 'macadamised'.

Everyone who travelled on Bristol's roads marvelled at how smooth and safe they were, and MacAdam was soon put in charge of roads all over England. His ideas quickly spread throughout Britain, Europe and the USA.

MacAdam travelled around the country researching the roads, with his giant Newfoundland dog often running alongside his carriage. He used all his own money on his road experiments and travels. Parliament did eventually give him some payment, and a knighthood in old age, which he didn't accept but instead passed on to his son. His name lives on in the word 'tarmac'.

MacAdam's ideas spread around the world. This advert shows a French road being built.

THOMAS TELFORD
A STAR BUILDING ENGINEER

BORN Westerkirk, Scotland, 9 August 1757
DIED London, 2 September 1834
AGE 77 years

Thomas Telford was the brilliant engineer who worked out how to build canals, bridges and roads across valleys, rivers and mountains. This enabled the factories of the Industrial Revolution to receive and transport raw materials and finished goods across Britain.

Born the son of a shepherd, Thomas Telford spent his early life as a farm boy. His first wages came from herding cows, for which he received some meat, stockings and money for clogs (shoes).

When Thomas was 14 he was apprenticed to a stonemason and began to learn the principles of building. He worked his way up in jobs around the country, and in 1790 he was given the

job of building a bridge over the River Severn. This was followed by the task of building a canal across a high valley. Telford's solution was to design an amazing aqueduct, a raised bridge made from strong cast iron plates fixed in masonry. It was the longest, highest aqueduct in Britain and was called the Pontcysyllte Aqueduct (Welsh for 'connecting bridge'). People in the valley found it a wondrous sight to see boats floating by high above their heads.

Telford became a renowned builder of bridges, canals, docks and roads. He designed the Menai Suspension Bridge, then the world's longest suspension bridge, which linked Anglesey to Wales for the first time over the dangerous waters of the Menai Straits.

All about canals

Before the advent of railways, the most efficient way to connect the mines, factories and ports of the Industrial Revolution was by canal. A canal is an artificial waterway, a deep trough cut from the earth and built to contain water. The great British engineers of the 18th century designed and built a canal system that spread right across the country between industrial towns and ports.

Thomas Telford's great contribution to the Industrial Revolution was to work out how to transport things the speediest way, by using new building techniques which were stronger and safer than ever before. 🏴

The Menai Suspension Bridge was one of Thomas Telford's finest achievements.

SIR GEORGE CAYLEY
THE FATHER OF FLIGHT

BORN Scarborough,
27 December 1773
DIED Scarborough,
15 December 1857
AGE 83 years

In 1903 the Wright Brothers achieved the world's first powered manned flight. However, they declared they could not have done it without using the research of Sir George Cayley, a great British engineering mind who discovered the basic principles of flight 50 years before.

Cayley was a baronet who lived in a grand home, Brompton Hall near Scarborough. When he wasn't making speeches in parliament, he was busy engineering new machines. He designed an airship, an early form of caterpillar track, and even invented an artificial limb and a gunpowder engine. He saw the world's first railway crash and immediately designed both passenger seatbelts and the cowcatcher, a kind of bumper fitted on the front of trains to make them safer.

Cayley's main interest was in flying. He studied birds to work out how they could fly without flapping their wings continuously, and did experiments with wing shapes on the staircase of his house. Then he set about building a glider from linen sheets, canes and string. He persuaded his coachman, John Appleby, to sit in it as the world's first test pilot. Then his other employees pulled on ropes to move the glider down a slope. It launched into the air and flew 275 m before it crashed. Appleby got out unhurt but is said to have resigned from his job on the spot, complaining that he had been hired to drive, not fly!

Cayley laid the foundations of aeronautics by discovering the principles

Cayley remembered

Sir George Cayley was for many years one of the forgotten pioneers of British engineering, more famous in the USA than in his own country. But his work has gradually become better known and celebrated. A replica of his glider was made for the celebration of 100 years of flight in 2003. Like many successful British engineers, Cayley never stopped questioning, inventing and testing new ideas all his life.

16

Sir George Cayley had an enquiring mind and was always working on new ideas.

of lift and thrust that keep an aeroplane aloft. He worked out the principles of controlling a plane, too, using wings and a tail. If there had been such a thing as a lightweight engine in his lifetime, he could quite possibly have beaten the Wright Brothers to fly a powered heavier-than-air flying machine! 🇬🇧

17

GEORGE STEPHENSON
THE DEVELOPER OF THE STEAM LOCOMOTIVE

BORN Wylam,
  Northumberland,
  9 June 1781
DIED Chesterfield,
  12 August 1848
AGE 67 years

George Stephenson became one of the most famous Britons of the 19th century. His celebrity was due to his steam locomotives, which hit the headlines and triggered the building of railways all over the country.

At the age of 14, George Stephenson was working at Killingworth Colliery. He only taught himself to read and write by going to night school. He was soon recognised as the best engine-mender in the colliery, and by the age of 31 he was in charge of all the colliery engines.

In 1814 Stephenson built his first steam locomotive, to pull coal wagons from the colliery. Then he persuaded the Stockton and Darlington Railway Company to build a steam locomotive

The coming of the railways

Railways quickly spread and soon replaced coach travel. Canals, too, eventually fell out of use. Railways were faster and more reliable than either form of transport. Not everybody welcomed them, though. Some saw them as dangerous and dirty. In fact, on the day the Liverpool and Manchester Railway opened, Stephenson's *Rocket* knocked over and killed a member of parliament, William Huskisson, at the opening ceremony in 1830.

passenger railway. His first railway engine, *Locomotion*, was the first public steam engine in the world to carry goods and people. The opening day of the railway attracted a great crowd, and by the time *Locomotion* reached its destination there were 600 people crowded in it, or hanging onto its wagons! Stephenson worked with his son Robert to build a faster locomotive, the *Rocket*. In 1829 it travelled at an amazing 48 km/h to win £500 in a famous race with other locomotive designs. It caused a great stir, and soon became the model for steam locomotives all over the world.

The success of the *Rocket* made Stephenson a rich man. He used some of his money to help the miners he had grown up with by paying for schools for miners' children, libraries, night schools and music clubs. He carried on inventing all his life, including more engines, a miner's lamp, and even a special glass tube to make his cucumbers grow straight! He was a natural engineer, not well-educated, but hugely talented and curious.

What made the Rocket so successful and speedy was the revolutionary design of its boiler.

ROBERT STEPHENSON
'A CHIP OFF THE OLD BLOCK'

BORN Willington Quay,
Newcastle,
16 October 1803
DIED London,
12 October 1859
AGE 55 years

Robert Stephenson was George Stephenson's only son. He helped his father build the *Rocket* that made international headlines, and though he is less famous nowadays than his father, he is often said to have been the true brains behind the *Rocket*'s success.

Robert Stephenson was born while his father was working at Killingworth Colliery. His mother died when he was only three. As his father grew more successful he was able to pay for Robert to go to school in Newcastle. The young Stephenson rode to school every day on a donkey, and was teased by the other boys for having a local accent. But he shone at school and soon followed in his father's footsteps as an engineer.

For a while the young Stephenson went to work in Colombia, South America, as an engineer in gold and silver mines. When he returned he became internationally famous for his long-spanned iron bridges and viaducts (bridges that carry railways). His best-known construction was the Britannia Bridge over the Menai Straits in Wales, and he also built the Victoria Bridge over the St Lawrence river at Montreal, Canada. He began to use steel girders on iron bridges for the first time, though his designs did not always perform well. One of his bridges collapsed while a train was crossing in 1847.

Stephenson's company became the world's leading locomotive maker,

Richard Trevithick

While Robert Stephenson was in South America he met Cornish engineer **RICHARD TREVITHICK** (1771-1833), a friend of his father's who had run out of money. Stephenson generously paid for him to get back to Britain. Trevithick experimented with early steam engine design, and George Stephenson later said that these experiments were vital to the success of his own steam locomotives. Trevithick is often regarded as the true 'father of the railways'.

supplying trains all over the globe. He even found time to be a member of parliament, and helped in the work of both his father and his friend Isambard Kingdom Brunel (see pages 24-25).

Robert Stephenson founded a company that supplied locomotives to railways around the world.

JOSEPH PAXTON
GARDENER AND BUILDER

BORN Milton Bryan,
3 August 1803
DIED Sydenham,
8 June 1865
AGE 61 years

Joseph Paxton designed the Crystal Palace, one of the most famous buildings in the 19th century world. It was the first prefabricated building, put together from pre-made parts.

Paxton was the seventh son of a farmer. As a boy he worked on a farm but ran away when he was beaten and starved. He lied about his age and got a job as a garden boy for a big house near Woburn, where he set about teaching himself all there was to know about gardening. At the age of 19 he designed his first lake.

Eventually he was appointed head gardener at Chatsworth, home of the Duke of Devonshire. He was soon managing all of the Duke's estates – designing gardens, creating lakes and building greenhouses to provide exotic fruit and flowers for the Duke's houses. Paxton always thought big. He designed and built the Great Conservatory at Chatsworth, at the time the largest glass building in the world.

In 1837 Paxton was given a cutting from a lily plant discovered in the Amazon rainforest. Nobody had been able to make the plant flower, but it thrived when Paxton designed a heated pool for it at Chatsworth. The leaves grew almost 3.6 m wide, and he tested how strong they were by getting his young daughter Annie to stand on them. He realised that the network of ribbed veins under the

A moveable building

The Crystal Palace building design was innovative because it was cheap and quick to build. All the parts of the building could be made in great numbers and then assembled on any site. It could be taken down, too. The Crystal Palace itself was moved out of Hyde Park to Sydenham once the exhibition ended. It was badly damaged by fire in 1936 and eventually demolished during World War II, because enemy planes were using it as a landmark to guide them to London.

leaves gave them their strength, and it gave him the idea for his most famous building, the Crystal Palace. He reportedly scribbled the design on scrap paper, but it was chosen over 245 other designs to be built in Hyde Park for the Great Exhibition, a huge public event held in 1851. It was basically a beautiful giant greenhouse, with nearly 300,000 panes of glass, 330 huge iron columns and 38.6 km of guttering.

Paxton was knighted, and later became a member of parliament. He also published gardening magazines and designed stately homes. His building design was copied in Europe and the USA, and inspired the prefabricated building methods that we use today.

Paxton's Crystal Palace was the showcase of Britain's Great Exhibition in 1851.

ISAMBARD KINGDOM BRUNEL
ALL-ROUND ENGINEER

BORN Portsmouth,
9 April 1806
DIED London,
15 September 1859
AGE 53 years

Isambard Kingdom Brunel is one of the most famous British engineers of all time. He achieved lots of engineering firsts, and his bridges, railway tunnels and stations are still in use today.

Brunel's father, Marc Brunel, was a famous engineer who came to England from France to escape the French Revolution. The young Brunel was well educated, and at 20 he began work for his father, who was building a tunnel under the River Thames at Rotherhithe. It was dangerous work, as the tunnel regularly flooded with river water. In fact Brunel nearly died when he was hurled from a tunnelling platform by a flash flood. He was knocked unconscious, but luckily was washed to the end of the tunnel and up a stairway, where he was pulled out, badly injured. The tunnel was eventually completed and is still used today on the London Underground between Rotherhithe and Wapping.

When Brunel was 26 he became Chief Engineer on the new Great Western Railway, which ran between London and Bristol. He came up with lots of innovative ideas to overcome obstacles on the railway route, including the world's longest underground railway tunnel at the time – the Box Tunnel – and Bristol Temple Meads Station, both

The idea that didn't work

Even the most successful engineers sometimes have ideas that don't work. Brunel's failed project was an 'atmospheric railway'. The idea was that trains would be pulled along by pumps sucking air through railway tunnels. A section of atmospheric railway was built in Devon and trains did run for a time. But they broke down regularly, and on those occasions third-class passengers had to get out and push. The leather flaps used to seal the pipes were eaten by rats, and after a few months the railway closed.

24

of which are still in use. Brunel became a famously recognisable figure as he strode about supervising his building projects, always wearing a tall hat and smoking a cigar. By the time he died he had engineered over 18,000 km of railway around the world.

Brunel's other big claims to fame were his revolutionary steamship designs. He built three giant steamships to travel across the Atlantic between Britain and the USA. The first one, the *Great Western*, sailed in 1838, and was the world's biggest steamship at that time. His second design, the *Great Britain*, was the first iron-hulled, propeller-driven ship to cross the Atlantic.

Brunel's third ship, the *Great Eastern*, was even bigger and more cutting-edge, but the strain of trying to get it built was fatal for Brunel, never a healthy man after his tunnel accident. While watching the *Great Eastern* do her sea trials in 1859, he had a stroke and died ten days later. One of his most famous project designs, the Clifton Suspension Bridge in Bristol, was built after his death, so he never saw it finished. 🇬🇧

The great 'IKB' poses with tall hat and cigar in front of the launching chains of the Great Eastern.

SIR HENRY BESSEMER
MAN OF STEEL

BORN Charlton,
Hertfordshire,
19 January 1813
DIED London,
15 March 1898
AGE 85 years

Henry Bessemer worked out how to make cheap steel, a lighter and stronger metal than iron. Through his invention, modern machines and buildings became possible – including steel ships, cars, aeroplanes and skyscrapers.

Bessemer became a 'grand old man' of engineering, giving lectures on his work.

Bessemer's father was an engineer who set up a metal type business (in those days printers used metal letters to print words). The young Bessemer was allowed to experiment with the molten metal used to make the letters, and loved to model it into different shapes. He was fascinated by machinery and often went to watch the flour mill at work in his village, or sneaked into his father's premises to watch the type being made.

Bessemer began to come up with a number of engineering ideas, and made his fortune by inventing a machine to create fine brass powder used to make gold paint, which was very popular in decorations of the time. He kept the machine a closely-guarded secret and only a few trusted people were allowed to work it. He began to experiment with metals, and got interested in steel-making when he was trying to find ways to make better guns.

At the time, there were two types of iron – cast iron and wrought iron. Both materials were full of impurities and took a lot of work to make them usable. The only material to be called steel was made by slowly adding carbon to wrought iron. This was an unreliable and labour-intensive method that only produced small quantities of the metal. Bessemer invented a converter, a furnace that turned molten iron into steel by blasting it with air. The converter was named after him, and enabled the modern steel industry to grow.

Like many of the famous engineers in this book, Bessemer invented a number of other things besides his 'big idea'. He built a telescope, worked out a new way to polish diamonds and even built a ship designed to overcome seasickness. It was tried out on the English Channel, but didn't work. Luckily, his steel-making converter was much more successful. 🏴

Steel is everywhere

With Bessemer's invention, steel became cheaper to make than iron. It was lighter in weight and also stronger, so it was ideal for everything from ships and railway tracks to building structures. Many future engineering developments would have been impossible without it. Next time you pass the building site of a large building, see if you can spot steel girders being used to create a strong building frame. And when you go to a Victorian railway station, look for the ironwork used in buildings before Bessemer came up with his new method of steel-making. The next step in steel-making was to combine steel with harder metals to create an alloy (combination) able to withstand big forces and high speeds.

SIR JOSEPH BAZALGETTE
THE MAN WHO CLEANED UP LONDON

BORN Enfield,
28 March 1819
DIED London,
15 March 1891
AGE 71 years

Joseph Bazalgette rebuilt London's sewage system. His pioneering civil engineering work saved many thousands of lives and formed the basis of London's sanitation today.

Bazalgette was the son of a captain in the Royal Navy, and, like his friend Isambard Kingdom Brunel, his family were originally from France. He began his career working as a railway engineer, and set up his own engineering firm.

In London at the time, the old system for getting rid of sewage was breaking down. The population was growing fast and the introduction of flushing toilets made the situation worse. Sewage was overflowing into the streets and running directly into the Thames, which was so polluted that no creature could survive in its waters. Cholera epidemics began to kill many thousands in London, but people mistakenly thought the disease was spread by 'foul air', not dirty water.

With the help of Brunel, Bazalgette got the job of looking after the sewers (after his predecessor in the job had died of 'fatigue and anxiety'). He proposed plans to build a new system using many miles of enclosed underground brick sewers to take waste away to the Thames Estuary, downstream from the city. In 1858, a particularly warm summer led to the 'Great Stink' when the smell of sewage overwhelmed the city, and this persuaded parliament to support Bazalgette's scheme.

Cholera – the invisible disease

In Victorian times people thought that cholera was caused by 'miasma' – foggy polluted air. There was certainly a lot of that in industrial London, but it did not carry cholera, which in fact was caught from drinking filthy water. Bazalgette's new sewage system did not cover London's East End, which still had sewage-polluted streets and water supplies. So when that area alone was ravaged by cholera in 1866, people began to realise that dirty water was the culprit.

A cartoon of the 1860s shows Bazalgette's face on one of his sewer pipes snaking around London.

The banks of the Thames became huge building sites as they were turned into giant embankments hiding the sewers beneath. Over 3.5 million tonnes of earth were excavated to build the sewers, and a number of pumping stations were built to help pump the water along. By the time Bazalgette died, the raging cholera epidemics and stinking streets of London were a memory. 🏴

SIR JOSEPH WHITWORTH
THE MAN WHO MADE THE TOOLS

BORN Stockport,
21 December 1803
DIED Monte Carlo,
22 January 1887
AGE 83 years

It's no good having fantastic engineering ideas without the tools to do the job! That's where Joseph Whitworth came in. He was the first person to develop tools that would make very accurate machinery.

Whitworth was born the son of a schoolmaster who was also a dissenter, which meant he questioned the recognised religion of the time and followed a different religious path. Whitworth's dissenter education was very practical, and also questioned accepted ideas, which perhaps contributed to his later achievements. When he was 14 he was apprenticed in a factory to a cotton-spinner. Soon he was studying the factory's machinery and working out how he could improve it.

Whitworth decided to try to be a mechanic. He went to Manchester and then to London, where he worked under some of the greatest engineering minds of the time. While he was there he helped to build the first calculating machine, the forerunner of the modern computer. He knew that the engineers he worked with wanted tools that were much more precise, and equipment such as screws that were all the same size, but no-one had yet made this happen.

Whitworth went back to Manchester and set up his own company. His most important innovation was to devise a way to make flat surfaces on metal with great accuracy. This enabled him to make engineering tools that could be used for precise work. He also devised standard sizes for screws, and soon these sizes were used in railways all over the world.

Handmade no longer

Although Whitworth did not create grand railways or steamships, he invented the machine tools that made them possible. Before his innovations, parts were individually made for each job, and not with any great accuracy. His precision tools meant that parts could be made exactly the same over and over again in factories, and the same tools could be used for lots of different projects.

Whitworth died a very wealthy man, and like many of the engineers in this book he donated lots of his wealth to help educate the poor. University buildings and an art gallery are still named after him today. He was said to be a difficult man – a perfectionist who demanded the best. He was certainly determined enough to change engineering forever. 🇬🇧

Sir Joseph Whitworth used his fortune to help educate the poor.

SIR CHARLES PARSONS
INVENTOR OF THE STEAM TURBINE

BORN London,
13 June 1854
DIED Jamaica,
11 February 1931
AGE 76 years

Sir Charles Parsons's invention of the steam turbine made cheap plentiful electricity possible. On the ocean, it brought about fast warships, which played a vital part in the world wars.

Although born in London, Charles Parsons grew up in a castle in Ireland. His father collected steam-powered machines and let his son experiment with them in the castle workshop. After attending university, Parsons turned his attention to improving steam engines. At this time they were very large and noisy, and tended to vibrate a lot as their pistons drove up and down. Parsons realised that a machine with parts that went round – a turbine – could be used to convert steam into electricity smoothly. In his invention, the steam turned turbine blades that drove an electrical generator. This new innovation brought about the spread of electric street lighting in

many British towns, and was soon adopted in electricity power stations worldwide.

At the same time, Parsons worked on marine steam turbines. First he experimented with a model boat towed on the end of a fishing rod. Then he built a full-sized boat, called the *Turbinia*. Three turbines drove propellers that pushed the ship through the water.

In 1897 he decided to show off his new invention by gatecrashing Queen Victoria's inspection of the Royal Navy fleet at Spithead. His boat zigzagged between the warships, too fast for anyone to catch. Luckily for him, the delighted

congratulations of the Royal watchers saved him from getting into big trouble! Soon afterwards the Navy adopted his idea and turbine-driven warships became standard.

Parsons's design for the steam turbine was brilliant, and wasn't improved upon for many years. He was given a knighthood and many awards for his lifetime of engineering work. 🏴

Parsons's launch Turbinia on its sea trials. When built it was the fastest ship afloat.

SIR HENRY ROYCE
CAR AND AERO-ENGINE DESIGNER

BORN Alwalton,
27 March 1863
DIED Cheshire,
22 April 1933
AGE 70 years

The Rolls-Royce is one of the world's most famous cars, and Rolls-Royce aero engines have powered many of the world's aeroplanes. The co-owner of Rolls-Royce was Henry Royce, a great innovator who had one of the toughest childhoods of anyone in this book.

Royce's father was a miller but, sadly, his business failed. The family moved to London, and when Henry was nine his father died in poverty in a Poor House, a bleak kind of government institution for those too poor to live anywhere else. As a result, Royce only had one year of schooling and earned what money he could from bird-scaring, selling newspapers on the street and delivering mail. His aunt paid for him to take an apprenticeship on the Great Northern Railway, but when she could no longer help out he had to leave. He tried to educate himself as best he could by going to night school.

Sir Henry Royce standing next to one of his most famous creations, the 'Roller'.

Royce was interested in electricity, and he eventually took a job working on theatre and street lights. He saved up £20, enough money to set up his own lighting company, and his ability to improve on existing lighting designs soon brought him success.

In the early 1900s motor cars began to interest Henry Royce. He decided he could improve on the one he had bought, and built his own car in the corner of his workshop. He went on to build three two-cylinder cars, one for himself and two for his friends. One of these friends introduced him to Charles Rolls, a car salesman with a London showroom. He agreed to sell the cars provided they were fitted with four cylinders and were given the name Rolls-Royce. The two set up in business together, and the car became world-renowned for its smooth-running reliability, luxury and performance. As well as cars, the company built aero engines used in both world wars. Rolls-Royce engines powered Spitfires, Hurricanes and Lancaster bombers in World War II.

Royce was a perfectionist who insisted on checking all new designs done by the engineers in his factory. It was his insistence on high standards that made Rolls-Royce such a successful company.

Rolls-Royce – luxury on the road

The Rolls-Royce, nicknamed the 'Roller', became a byword for the most luxurious car in existence. Kings and queens, multi-millionaires and presidents all wanted to be driven in the best car possible – a Rolls-Royce. Though Royce was actually knighted for his major contribution to aircraft engines, he is probably more famous for the classy car he developed. A modern Rolls-Royce costs many thousands of pounds, an unimaginable amount for the young Royce when he was a poor London street boy.

SIR NIGEL GRESLEY
THE DESIGNER OF RECORD-BREAKING TRAINS

BORN Edinburgh,
19 June 1876
DIED Derbyshire,
5 April 1941
AGE 64 years

Nigel Gresley became one of Britain's most successful steam locomotive designers. His most famous design, *Mallard*, still holds the world speed record for steam trains.

Gresley was born the son of a vicar. He went to Marlborough College, a private school, where he came top in science and developed a flair for mechanical drawings. On leaving school, he took up a railway apprenticeship, and learnt his trade under the most skilled engineers of the day.

Eventually Gresley was made Chief Mechanical Engineer of the London and North Eastern Railway (LNER), which ran passenger trains up the east coast of Britain. There he designed a whole group of locomotives called the A4 Class. They were renowned for being fast and innovative, and they had an up-to-date aerodynamic shape. The elegance of Gresley's A4s caught the public imagination, and the speed records they broke made them world famous.

Gresley's earlier locomotive, the A3 class *Flying Scotsman,* was the first engine officially to do over 100 mph (160 kph) pulling a passenger train. In addition, the A4 *Mallard* still holds the record as the fastest steam train in the world, reaching 201 kph in 1938. It can still be seen at the National Railway Museum in York. In the 1930s there was no speed limit for trains, which could go as fast as their drivers and firemen could make them.

The celebrity train

Gresley's loco the *Flying Scotsman* became a national icon, a train with celebrity-status. Everybody had heard of it. Famous paintings were made of it, and it was used to publicise Britain and make her citizens feel proud of their country's engineering heritage. It came to epitomise British steam railway achievement, and when diesel trains took over the country's networks, it evoked great nostalgia for the 'Age of Steam'.

One of Gresley's streamlined A4 'Pacific' class locomotives, a sister to Mallard.

Gresley's locomotives worked on into the late 1950s, when they were gradually replaced by diesel locomotives. A number of them have been carefully preserved by railway enthusiasts.

LORD NUFFIELD
THE CREATOR OF AFFORDABLE CARS

BORN Worcester,
10 October 1877
DIED Henley-on-
Thames, 22 August
1963
AGE 85 years

Lord Nuffield founded Morris Motors, which at one time made half the cars on the roads in Britain. He is also famous for donating over £30 million to charity, in particular to the Nuffield Foundation.

Lord Nuffield's real name was William Morris. When he was young his family moved to Oxford. He left school at 14 to repair bicycles, and with £4 set up a bicycle repair shop in his father's

Lord Nuffield driving one of his own cars, built at the huge factory in Cowley, Oxford.

garden shed. Later he worked on motorbikes and then opened a garage selling and repairing cars. He admired the cheap cars being made in the USA by Henry Ford (1863-1947), and decided to build his own version. He gave his first car the name Morris, and called his company Morris Motors.

Morris built his cars in an empty building in Cowley, Oxford. Eventually his Cowley factory grew into one of the biggest car-producing centres in Europe. Morris cars were sold worldwide and ranged from the family Morris Minor to the sporty MG. Morris became a very rich and famous man, and was given a peerage

Cars for everyone

Lord Nuffield took his inspiration from **HENRY FORD** (1863-1947), who was mass-producing cars in the USA that were cheap enough for ordinary people to buy. Prior to Ford and Morris Motors, cars were luxury goods for the rich. By the time Lord Nuffield died, cars were much more common in Britain. Today it's very hard to imagine life without them.

in 1938, taking the name of Nuffield from the village where he lived. But his fame made him the target of an infamous failed kidnap attempt in 1938. A blackmailer planned to pose as a journalist, kidnap him and force him to pay for his release, but an accomplice informed the police and they ambushed the kidnapper.

Lord Nuffield decided to use his wealth to help those less well-off than himself. He donated money to charitable causes around the world, especially for medical research, and he set up the Nuffield Foundation with a huge gift of £10 million, to support good causes long after his own life was over. Though fabulously wealthy, Lord Nuffield only drove his own small cars, content with what he himself had created.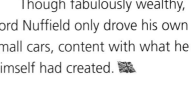

SIR HARRY RICARDO
A LEADING ENGINE DESIGNER

BORN London,
26 January 1885
DIED Midhurst, Sussex,
18 May 1974
AGE 89 years

Sir Harry Ricardo was one of the foremost engine designers of the 20th century. He developed car and aeroplane engines, and his work helped Britain to win two world wars.

Ricardo was born to a wealthy family of engineers. It's likely he may have been one of the first people in Britain to see a motor car, as his grandfather bought one in 1898. Ricardo was expected to go into his family's civil engineering business (civil engineers design big structures such as buildings, roads and water supply systems). But instead he decided to be a mechanical engineer (working on machines with lots of components, such as engines).

When Ricardo went to Cambridge University he entered a competition to

design the machine that would go the furthest on a quart (one litre) of fuel. His motorcycle design was by far the heaviest entered, but it won. He began to experiment with engines and when he graduated, he set up a company at Shoreham-by-Sea near Southampton. He patented a revolutionary two-stroke engine, and went on to design the engines used for the first successful tanks. Thousands of his Mark V tank engines were built for wartime use, and helped Britain win World War I.

All his life Ricardo experimented and drove forward the world's engine industry. He helped to design the world's first diesel-powered car, and his improvements made high-speed diesel travel possible. He set up Ricardo

The secrets of fuel

Ricardo realised that an engine relied for its performance on the type of fuel it used. He discovered how important the make-up of fuel was, and this led to fuels being graded in different ways. The discoveries led to a big reduction in the amount of fuel needed by aeroplanes. Flying long distances became possible for the first time.

Consulting Engineers, and after his death it still remains one of the world's foremost engine research centres, involved in many record-breaking developments. In 1986 it adapted the engine of the *Voyager*, the first plane ever to fly non-stop around the world without refuelling.

British tanks go into action during World War I. Sir Harry Ricardo designed their engines.

SIR FRANK WHITTLE
THE INVENTOR OF THE JET ENGINE

BORN Coventry,
1 June 1907
DIED Maryland, USA,
9 August 1996
AGE 89 years

Frank Whittle was one of the foremost aeronautical engineers of the 20th century. His ideas led to the development of the jet engine, which made fast jet air travel possible.

Frank Whittle's father owned a small engineering company. As a child, Frank often helped his father in the workshop. When he was four, Frank was given a model aeroplane that sparked his lifelong interest in flying.

In 1923 Whittle joined the Royal Air Force (RAF) and, while training to be a pilot, he developed his ideas on future aeroplane design. He saw rocket-propulsion as the way forward and developed the idea of a turbo-jet engine. In a jet engine, air gets sucked in through a compressor, a series of vanes that spin round, squeezing the air into a combustion chamber. Here it is mixed with fuel and ignited, making hot gases shoot backwards through the blades of a turbine that spin round, turning the compressor. The gases shoot out of the back of the aeroplane, powering it forwards.

Initially Whittle's idea was rejected by the RAF as 'impractical', and Whittle spent years trying to get his ideas accepted by the British. Meanwhile the German aeroplane industry took advantage of his work, and would have developed jet-powered fighter planes more quickly than Britain had Adolf Hitler not decided against the idea. In 1944 Whittle's Gloster Meteor became the first jet plane ever to work in an operational air force squadron.

Jet over propellor

Prior to jet engines aeroplanes were driven by piston engines that drove propellors at the front of a plane. Jet engines provided much greater power and speed, and so transformed the role of fighter planes. A pilot who flew one of the first jet-powered planes described the experience as feeling 'like angels flying'.

WHITTLE W1X, 1941

Sir Frank Whittle stands in front of his prototype jet engine, the 'WU' (Whittle Unit).

After the war Whittle still found it hard to get his ideas through to production, and he had to battle to get the finance to build his engines, and to get recognition for his work. Yet now jet engines power passenger planes and jet fighters throughout the world.

LORD FOSTER
MODERN BUILDING INNOVATOR

BORN Manchester, 1 June 1935

Norman Foster's company, Foster and Partners, is responsible for some of the world's most famous and unusual modern buildings and bridges.

Although Norman Foster is an architect by training, he heads up a company that works with teams of engineering designers to create groundbreaking new structures. Foster left school when he was 16 and only later went to Manchester University to train in Architecture and City Planning. He did not come from a wealthy background, and he paid his way through university by taking lots of part-time jobs, including selling ice-cream and being a nightclub bouncer. After university he co-founded some influential architecture companies, and developed groundbreaking ideas for buildings that took the environment into consideration, being designed in such a way as to save on power use.

Computers are now a crucial tool in engineering design. Foster and his engineering teams work out ways to make 'intelligent buildings', with aspects such as heating run by complex computer systems. The structures also look hi-tec and futuristic. His projects have included skyscrapers around the world, such as the 'Gherkin' in London, which gets its nickname from its unusual shape. The buildings are often made from repeated shapes – 'modular units' – which are prefabricated and then brought to the building site.

Like many of the innovators in this book, Norman Foster sometimes runs into controversy because his designs are groundbreaking and unusual. However,

Engineering and the environment

Norman Foster puts the emphasis on environmentally-friendly design, a strand of engineering that was not a concern in the past but is now very important. Structures must work without using up too much of the earth's resources. His buildings run on unusual fuels such as vegetable oil, and try to use more natural air ventilation instead of expensive fuel-hungry air-conditioning.

his Millenium Bridge over London's River Thames made headlines not because of its looks but because of its engineering problems. It wobbled alarmingly when lots of people walked over it, and it had to be altered to solve the difficulty. Even with powerful computer programs at their disposal, engineering designers sometimes take a while to get ideas right.

Norman Foster was given a peerage for his work in 1990. He and his teams approach each project with fresh new ideas. Like many of the engineers of the past, they never stop thinking of new ways to make life better.

> **Norman Foster heads teams of engineers and architects creating new buildings.**

Glossary

Aerodynamic A smooth shape that slips easily through the air without much resistance.

Aeronautical engineering The design, building and repairing of flying machines.

Age of Reason A period during the 18th century in Britain when many philosophers and scientists were coming up with new inventions and theories.

Apprentice Someone who trains as they work, under the guidance of a more senior person.

Aqueduct A raised bridge made to carry a canal.

Canal A man-made waterway.

Civil engineering The design and building of big publicly-used structures such as buildings, roads and water supply systems.

Converter A kind of furnace used to turn molten iron into steel.

Cylinder The central part of an engine – a metal casing with a piston inside it.

Diesel A type of fuel used to run a diesel engine.

Engineer Someone who designs and works with machinery or with structures such as bridges or buildings.

Furnace A kind of large industrial oven, used to produce enough heat to melt material such as iron ore.

Girder A strong piece of steel used to make a rigid framework for a bridge or building.

Hooke's joint A joint in a rigid rod that allows that rod to bend in any direction. It is used in the driveshaft of vehicles to transmit power from the engine to the wheels.

Horsepower A measurement used to describe the power of an engine.

Industrial Revolution A period in the 18th and 19th centuries when factories sprang up across Britain, using new industrial methods to make large amounts of goods. Railways were built to transport goods and passengers.

Iron ore A mixture of minerals and rock dug from the ground, from which iron is extracted.

Jet engine An engine that relies on jet propulsion to provide power. The propulsion comes from a jet of hot gases that shoot out of the back of the engine.

Knighthood An honour bestowed by the British monarch. A number of famous engineers have been given knighthoods for their contribution to British industry. They are entitled to call themselves 'Sir'.

Machine tools Tools used to manufacture machine parts.

Mass-production The making of many identical items in a factory.

Mechanical engineering The design, building and repairing of machinery.

Mechanism One particular working part of a machine.

Patent A legal licence that gives someone the sole right to manufacture an invention.

Peerage An honour bestowed by a monarch. Some famous engineers have been given peerages. They are entitled to call themselves 'Lord'.

Piston A section of an engine that moves up and down inside a cylinder.

Prefabricated Built by fitting together parts made at another location.

Propeller A set of blades that spin round, helping to power a boat or aircraft.

Pumping station A building housing machinery to help pump water round a sewage system.

Sewer A pipe that sewage runs through.

Smelting Burning coal with iron ore to make the iron ore melt, separating out the useful iron.

Steam engine An engine that uses pressurised steam to push a rod called a piston up and down inside a container called a cylinder.

Steam locomotive The front part of a train that runs using a steam engine.

Steamship A ship that runs on the power provided by steam engines.

Steel A strong lightweight metal made from treated iron.

Turbine A set of blades that spins inside an engine.

Viaduct A raised bridge made to carry a road or railway.

Watt A unit of electrical power.

Some useful websites

www.bbc.co.uk/history/historic_figures
A big database of famous people for you to search.

www.britainunlimited.com
All you need to know on the lives of 250 great Britons, including famous engineers.

www.spartacus.schoolnet.co.uk
Lots of biographies of famous engineers.

www.wikipedia.org
The Internet's amazing free encyclopedia, with lots of entries on British engineers and their work.

Note to parents and teachers:
Every effort has been made by the Publishers to ensure that the websites in this book are suitable for children, that they are of the highest educational value, and that they contain no inappropriate or offensive material. However, because of the nature of the Internet, it is impossible to guarantee that the contents of these sites will not be altered. We strongly advise that Internet access is supervised by a responsible adult.

SOME PLACES TO VISIT

Canal Trusts
Find your local Canal Trust by typing in 'Canal Trust' into a UK Internet search engine, or ask at your local tourist office.

Ironbridge Gorge Museum, Shropshire
This museum and the surrounding landscape will give you a sense of what it was like to live and work during the Industrial Revolution.

National Motor Museum, Beaulieu, Hampshire
A fabulous collection of vehicles in the grounds of a stately home.

National Railway Museum, York
The largest railway museum in the world.

Museum of the Great Western Railway, Swindon
Learn all about Isambard Kingdom Brunel's great railway achievements.

Science Museum, Kensington, London
Britain's biggest science museum.

SS Great Britain, Bristol Docks
Get on board Isambard Kingdom Brunel's steamship.

Steam railways
Check your local tourist office to find the nearest steam railway to you.

Index

These are the lists of contents for each title in *Great Britons*:

LEADERS
Boudica • Alfred the Great • Richard I • Edward I • Robert Bruce
Owain Glyndwr • Henry V • Henry VIII • Elizabeth I
Oliver Cromwell • The Duke of Marlborough • Robert Walpole
Horatio Nelson • Queen Victoria • Benjamin Disraeli
William Gladstone • David Lloyd George • Winston Churchill
Clement Attlee • Margaret Thatcher

CAMPAIGNERS FOR CHANGE
John Wycliffe • John Lilburne • Thomas Paine • Mary Wollstonecraft
William Wilberforce • Elizabeth Fry • William Lovett
Edwin Chadwick • Lord Shaftesbury • Florence Nightingale
Josephine Butler • Annie Besant • James Keir Hardie • Emmeline Pankhurst
Eleanor Rathbone • Ellen Wilkinson • Lord David Pitt • Bruce Kent
Jonathon Porritt • Shami Chakrabati

NOVELISTS
Aphra Behn • Jonathan Swift • Henry Fielding • Jane Austen
Charles Dickens • The Brontë Sisters • George Eliot • Lewis Carroll
Thomas Hardy • Robert Louis Stevenson • Arthur Conan Doyle
Virginia Woolf • D H Lawrence • J R R Tolkien • George Orwell
Graham Greene • William Golding • Ian McEwan • J K Rowling
Caryl Phillips • Andrea Levy • Zadie Smith
Monica Ali • Salman Rushdie

ARTISTS
Nicholas Hilliard • James Thornhill • William Hogarth
Joshua Reynolds • George Stubbs • William Blake • J M W Turner
John Constable • David Wilkie • Dante Gabriel Rossetti
Walter Sickert • Gwen John • Wyndham Lewis • Vanessa Bell
Henry Moore • Barbara Hepworth • Francis Bacon • David Hockney
Anish Kapoor • Damien Hirst

ENGINEERS
Robert Hooke • Abraham Darby • James Watt • John MacAdam
Thomas Telford • George Cayley • George Stephenson • Robert Stephenson
Joseph Paxton • Isambard Kingdom Brunel • Henry Bessemer
Joseph Bazalgette • Joseph Whitworth • Charles Parsons • Henry Royce
Nigel Gresley • Lord Nuffield • Harry Ricardo • Frank Whittle • Norman Foster

SCIENTISTS
John Dee • Robert Boyle • Isaac Newton • Edmond Halley • William Herschel
Michael Faraday • Charles Babbage • Mary Anning • Charles Darwin
Lord Kelvin • James Clerk Maxwell • Ernest Rutherford • Joseph Rotblat
Dorothy Hodgkin • Alan Turing • Francis Crick • Stephen Hawking
John Sulston • Jocelyn Bell Burnell • Susan Greenfield

SPORTING HEROES
WG Grace • Arthur Wharton • Kitty Godfree • Roger Bannister
Stirling Moss • Jackie Stewart • Bobby Moore • George Best
Gareth Edwards • Barry Sheene • Ian Botham • Nick Faldo
Torville and Dean • Lennox Lewis • Daley Thompson • Steve Redgrave
Tanni Grey-Thompson • Kelly Holmes • David Beckham • Ellen McArthur

MUSICIANS
William Byrd • Henry Purcell • George Frideric Handel • Arthur Sullivan
Edward Elgar • Henry Wood • Ralph Vaughan Williams • Noel Coward
Michael Tippet • Benjamin Britten • Vera Lynn
John Dankworth and Cleo Laine • Jacqueline Du Pre
Eric Clapton • Andrew Lloyd Webber • Elvis Costello
Simon Rattle • The Beatles • Courtney Pine • Evelyn Glennie